SMALL BUSINESS ACCOUNTING 101

The Financial Intelligence Needed For Success

"Some people dream of success, while other people get up every morning and make it happen"

—WAYNE HUIZENGA

CONTENTS

About The Author 1
Small Business Accounting 2
The Balance Sheet Introduction 3
The Chart Of Accounts Introduction 3
Long Term Liability Introduction 4
Income Statement Introduction 4
Financial Terms Introduction 5
Small Business Accounting Summary 6
The Balance Sheet 8
Accounting 101 The Balance Sheet 8
The Balance Sheet Assets 9
The Balance Sheet Liabilities 10
The Balance Sheet Equity 10
The Balance Sheet Summary 12
The Chart Of Accounts 14
Step 1: Set Up The Company 14
Step 2: Note Accounts Needed 15
Step 3: Set Up Account Numbers 16
Step 4: Review, Edit, Delete 17
Step 5: Grouping and Sub Accounts 17
Financial Terms 19
Financial Terms Balance Sheet 19
Financial Terms Income Statement 20
Financial Terms Cash Flow 22
Financial Terms Summary 23
The Income Statement 25
Accounting 101 The Income Statement 26
The Income Statement Financials 28
The Income Statement Summary 31
Long Term Liability 32
Long Term Liability Defined 33
Long Term Liability Managing 33
Long Term Liability Types 34

Long Term Liability Function 35
Long Term Liability Success 36
Long Term Liability Summary 37
Small Business Accounting 101 Conclusion 37
Additional Resources 39
Notes 40

ABOUT THE AUTHOR

Stephanie has a passion for helping people to improve their lives both personally and financially by learning new financial and personal self-help tools.

Her own personal journey has led to compiling this book that reveals many simple financial techniques that anyone can apply immediately for a powerful, positive money and business success transformation.

By the end of this book, you'll know how the need for personal self-improvement and knowledge determines the actions we should take moving forward for a better financial future.

SMALL BUSINESS ACCOUNTING

Introduction

*There is always space for improvement,
no matter how long you've been in the business.*
—Oscar De La Hoya

DO YOU UNDERSTAND THE TERMINOLOGY and processes involved in maintaining your business financial statements? As a small business owner, it's important to understand how accounting activities tie into your everyday operations.

Keeping track of your profits and expenses will indicate how well your business is doing and what you need to do to improve.

Even if you are able to hire a bookkeeper or accountant to handle your finances, it's good to have the basics of small business accounting down to oversee what is being done.

THE BALANCE SHEET INTRODUCTION

The balance sheet (B/S) shows all the liabilities, assets and net worth of the company and provides a snapshot of what is owed and what is owned.

If you have investors or are seeking a loan, you most likely will need to produce a balance sheet to show them why you and your company are worth their investment.

THE CHART OF ACCOUNTS INTRODUCTION

Learn how to set up a chart of accounts in QuickBooks. The QuickBooks accounting software is one of the most user friendly, forgiving accounting software programs available.

It is especially so when setting up the accounting chart of accounts. QuickBooks makes it easy.

LONG TERM LIABILITY INTRODUCTION

Long-term liability is a claim on the assets of a business and it has a major impact on the financial health of an organization over time.

This is especially true if the long-term liability for a company is poorly recorded and poorly managed.

Here we will show you how important these debts are for determining and preserving financial stability.

INCOME STATEMENT INTRODUCTION

This is also known as a profit and loss statement, and shows what your company has brought in and paid out. It also displays what your income has been over a certain period of time.

With the profit and loss statement, you will know whether or not your company is making or losing money - an important part of understanding accounting and bookkeeping principles.

You can determine which processes, services or products you need to enhance, and which ones you need to get rid of.

FINANCIAL TERMS INTRODUCTION

Assets

Assets are what you own or what is owed to you. This includes equipment, buildings, furniture and outstanding invoices (accounts receivable).

Liabilities

Liabilities are what you owe and other debts. This includes invoices you need to pay (accounts payable), payroll and taxes.

Net Worth

This is your assets minus your liabilities and is also known as your company's equity.

SMALL BUSINESS ACCOUNTING SUMMARY

These financial activities are crucial elements of any small business and should be prepared on a monthly or somewhat regular basis via professional bookkeeping services or the accountant or business owner. It should be reviewed to see where the company stands.

You may want to obtain a financial accounting program that can generate these documents for you at a moment's notice.

A financial accounting program can also help you design and prepare invoices, estimates and will keep all your financial records and information in one consolidated place for better recordkeeping.

The principles of small business accounting are not hard – it just requires due diligence and good reporting procedures.

Once you get over the initial hurdle and learning curve, keeping up with these accounting and bookkeeping basics will be a breeze!

If needed, there are classes available that teach business accounting 101, or you can have your outsourced bookkeeping services or your accountant show you the basics. The financial health of your company depends on it.

THE BALANCE SHEET

Know Where Your Money Is Going

*Money won't create success,
the freedom to make it will.*
—*Nelson Mandela*

WHAT DO YOU THINK OF when you hear the words balance sheet as a small business owner? The answer received most often is: I need to know where my money is going. So, let's use an extreme analogy for a moment. As a business owner, your business finances are your blood and your books are your veins and good bookkeeping keeps your business flowing.

ACCOUNTING 101 THE BALANCE SHEET

A big part of small business accounting 101 is the balance sheet. The balance sheet is the big-picture summary of how your business is doing at a moment in time, usually at the end of a month or year.

If you have investors or are seeking a loan, you most likely will need to produce a balance sheet to show them why you and your company are worth their investment.

A balance sheet has three main components: assets (the things you own), liabilities (the things you owe), and equity (the amount you and investors have put in).

For any small business owner it's essential Accounting 101 to understand all three of these categories in the balance sheet.

THE BALANCE SHEET ASSETS

Assets are everyone's favorite part of the business. Many different things can make up your business's assets, but the most common are:

- cash

- inventory
- accounts receivable

If you go beyond in accounting chart of accounts, you will learn about the more intangible kinds of assets.

THE BALANCE SHEET LIABILITIES

Liabilities are the things your business owes to others, including:

- accounts payable
- unpaid salaries
- deposits from customers

These may seem less exciting than your assets, but once you learn accounting 101 and grasp the balance sheet, you'll understand that both are equally important.

THE BALANCE SHEET EQUITY

On a company's balance sheet, equity refers to the amount of the funds contributed by the owners (also known as the stockholders) plus the retained earnings (or losses). This is also referred to as "shareholders' equity".

As you may guess from the name, your balance sheet requires that your assets, liabilities and equity all *balance*.

This means that your assets, totaled up, should be equal to your liabilities plus your equity. In general, this is also true on a smaller scale.

You pay cash or acquire an account payable to acquire inventory, so these transactions are equal. You invest a few thousand of your own dollars, increasing cash and increasing your equity at the same time.

That in essence is the crucial principle you need to understand about your balance sheet and accounting 101 the income statement - *assuming that each of your transactions is recorded correctly and transferred correctly to your balance sheet, everything should add up to the penny.*

Balance sheets therefore do two things for you as a business owner: they allow you to demonstrate to investors how strong your business is, and they allow you to keep an eye on the big picture and make sure your business is using money wisely.

THE BALANCE SHEET SUMMARY

Though the balance sheet is a key part of your business's accounting process, it is by no means the only thing you need to know.

As a small business owner it is essential that you understand how all these various financial parts of your business come together to give you the bigger picture of your businesses financial health.

If you need advice on your businesses financial health or are in need of professional bookkeeping services, we would love to talk to you.

THE CHART OF ACCOUNTS

How To Set Up The COA

An investment in knowledge pays the best interest.
—Benjamin Franklin

HOW DOES ONE GO ABOUT setting up the chart of accounts? Learning how to set up a chart of accounts is simple when using accounting software like QuickBooks. The QuickBooks software is one of the most popular and user friendly, forgiving accounting programs available out there. It is especially so when setting up the COA. QuickBooks makes it easy.

STEP 1: SET UP THE COMPANY

QuickBooks accounting software walks you through this process step by step. When given the option to choose an industry during the company set up process, choose the one that fits your company or the closest available. This will provide a relevant framework from which to build the individual company's chart of accounts.

STEP 2: NOTE ACCOUNTS NEEDED

Divide company accounts into the following categories and subcategories on paper. It also helps to give each account a unique name at this point.

1. Assets
2. Liabilities
3. Revenues
4. Expenses
5. Equity
6. Other
7. Suspense

The "other" account is for those revenues and expenses that do not relate directly to the business of the company.

These would include income from interest on notes receivable, or gain or loss on the sale of company assets.

The "suspense" account will hold any items that you are not sure how to record until you can determine how they should be reported.

STEP 3: SET UP ACCOUNT NUMBERS

This is an easy but necessary step. To number accounts, first select the company you are going to be working in.

From there go to edit> preferences> accounting> company preferences> use account numbers.

QuickBooks accounting software automatically sets number ranges for the various types of accounts.

STEP 4: REVIEW, EDIT, DELETE

Now you find yourself with a basic framework for a chart of accounts that you need to personalize to your company, and a list of accounts that need to be included in order to be specific to your company.

Compare the list you made in step 2 to the chart of accounts automatically generated by the program during the company set up process. Delete, edit, and add accounts as necessary to ensure the chart includes all of the accounts on your list.

To delete an account, click on the account in the chart of accounts, and then choose delete.

To change the name, simply click on edit instead of delete and type in the new name.

To add a new account, choose the "new" option rather than the "delete" or "edit" options.

STEP 5: GROUPING AND SUB ACCOUNTS

For income tax return purposes, certain accounts can be grouped, such as electricity, water, and gas under "Utilities." For management purposes, more detail is needed. QuickBooks accounting software allows for the use of sub-accounts for just this reason.

To create sub-accounts, go to company> chart of accounts> highlight the sub-account> select account> edit account> choose the "sub account of" option> then select the desired parent account.

Reports will show either parent account totals only, or they can show more detail that include parent account totals as well as each sub – account and its respective total.

Setting up a chart of accounts in QuickBooks does not have to be overwhelming. It may take a little time, but following these steps will ensure you get the best start and get it done as quickly as possible.

FINANCIAL TERMS

The Words Every Business Must Know

> *The true delight is in the*
> *finding out rather than in the knowing.*
> —Isaac Asimov

THE BEST WAY TO UNDERSTAND the most important bookkeeping and accounting definitions is to look at the three main financial statements. Work your way through each of these statements, making sure that you have a good understanding of the terms in bold and you will know how to keep score in your business. You win when there is profit at the end of the month or year, and when there is long term equity value when you are ready to cash out.

FINANCIAL TERMS BALANCE SHEET

Accounting 101 the balance sheet shows the value of your company as of a specific date such as the end of a month, quarter or year.

A comparative balance sheet compares one period to another and this is a way to monitor your progress.

The formula used to prepare the Balance Sheet is Assets -Liabilities = Shareholders (Owner's) Equity

Assets (Cash, Accounts Receivable, Inventory, Land, Building & Equipment) – What you *own*

 - **Liabilities** (Notes Payable, Accounts Payable) – What you *owe*

= **Owner's Equity (Retained Earnings** + Capital Stock) - What you *keep*.

FINANCIAL TERMS INCOME STATEMENT

Accounting 101 the income statement shows the aspect of accounting 101 where you keep track of what is coming in and going out of your business during a period of time like a month or a year.

Income/Revenue or Sales (Cash vs. Accrual Accounting determines when Income is recognized)

- Cost of Goods Sold – What it costs you to make your product or service
- Cost of Sales – Sales salaries, commission and expenses

= **Gross Profit** – Profit before expenses – You want this to be a positive number or it is a **Loss**

- **Expenses** (Rent, Heat, Payroll, etc.) – What it costs to operate your business

= Net Earnings before Taxes **(NEBT)**

- Taxes (Income Taxes)

= **Net Profit** - AKA The **Bottom Line** – This is why you are in business.

FINANCIAL TERMS CASH FLOW

The Cash Flow Statement or Cash Forecast or Source & Use of Funds is the final statement in small business accounting 101.

You use the cash flow statement to understand where your cash comes from, where it goes and to forecast how much cash you need to run the business.

Beginning Cash – Money in the bank

+ Accounts Receivable – Money owed to you by customers that has been **Invoiced**

+ Forecasted Sales – What your sales team expects to convert into cash

- Expenses – Forecasted expenses as shown on the income statement

= **Ending Cash** – What you have to work with to run the business

Recurring Revenue – This is the Holy Grail of business. Revenue you can count on every month like rent, maintenance, licenses, subscriptions, etc. It is one of the most valuable aspects of accounting 101.

Long Term Legacy Value – This is another way of saying retained earnings and it is the ultimate goal of a business owner to know how much your company is worth.

FINANCIAL TERMS SUMMARY

Accounting 101 financial terms is all about knowing how to keep score in your business.

You win when there is a positive number on the bottom line of the Income Statement (**Profit**), and when the **Retained Earnings** continues to grow and your **Long Term Equity Value** increase over time.

Use these terms and the financial statements as your guide to understanding accounting 101 as the way to keep score.

THE INCOME STATEMENT

Know How To Read And Interpret It

Invest three percent of your income in yourself (self-development) in order to guarantee your future..
—Brian Tracy

NOW I WANT TO DISCUSS THE IMPORTANCE for every business owner to comprehend how to read and interpret their income statement. This financial report is also known as the profit and loss statement, which is what you may know it better as. Recently, a small business owner asked for an hour of basic accounting consulting time to help her with here "out of control expenses."

To prepare for the meeting I asked her to send me her financial statements. Imagine my surprise when she said she doesn't have a bookkeeper and therefore has no small business accounting financial statements.

ACCOUNTING 101 THE INCOME STATEMENT

As mentioned above, we are focusing on the income statement in this section. Every business owner should be using their income statement to track revenues and expenses so that they can determine the operating performance of their business over a period of time.

SMBs (small to medium-sized businesses) should use their balance sheet and income statement to find out what areas of their business are over budget or under budget. Specific items that are causing unexpected expenditures can be pinpointed, such as phone, mail, print, or supply expenses.

Income statements can also track dramatic increases in product returns or cost of goods sold as a percentage of sales. They also can be used to determine income tax liability.

Your business's income statement is one of four key financial statements which most companies use to measure their profitability and over-all, financial stability. These four statements include the:

- balance sheet
- income statement (profit and loss statement)
- cash-flow statement
- statement of changes in equity

As we know from accounting 101 chart of accounts, the income statement is one of the most important financial statements for a business owner to keep an eye on.

From an overall accounting perspective, knowing how to read and interpret your income statement helps business owners to better formulate an intelligent business plan, as well as differentiating net income comparisons between specific periods of operation records.

This very important business financial statement compares the current year's income and expenses to those of the previous year. When this financial statement is read properly, the recorded data helps you to decipher whether or not your business is making money the way it should be.

The income statement gives you, as the business owner or bookkeeper/accountant, an idea as to what is making your business money and what is losing money.

THE INCOME STATEMENT FINANCIALS

The income statement measures a certain period of time in which a business operates including monthly, quarterly or annually.

Of course, your business never stops operating, but the income statement is a good comparison tool for figuring net income increase or decrease per statement period.

What is ideal for these comparisons is a steady net income growth realization. If you find there are more credits to debits, the business's net income increases. In other words, your business is doing well.

However, if there are more debits to credits, the business experienced a net loss, causing over all business assets to decreases. When this happens, your business is not doing so well.

When reading your business's profit and loss income statement keep in mind that the document will be broken down into several detailed parts.

This may sound intimidating but breaking the income statement into manageable chunks of information makes it easier for you to read and interpret the statement.

The important task of reading and interpreting the income statement is at the core of understanding your financial situation and the principles of accounting 101 financial terms. Your business's income statement should include separate sections on:

- income from continuing operations
- discontinued operation income
- unusual or infrequent income
- income from change in accounting principles
- net income
- other income
- earnings per share

Revenues from the continuing operations section is the most important part of any business's income statement. Results from this section can predict your company's future earnings when compared to past continuing operations net income or net losses.

The items included in your business's continuing operations involve revenues from sales of your company's products or services, costs of the products or services, operating expenses such as utilities, rent and HVAC, income tax expenses and gains or losses of revenue during business operations.

THE INCOME STATEMENT SUMMARY

In small business accounting 101 the income statement is a fundamental statement that all business owners should grasp and know how to use to track their businesses revenues as well as deductible expenses.

This will equip them with the necessary information to determine the operating performance of their business over a period of time.

LONG TERM LIABILITY

What It Is And Why You Should Care

*Debt is one person's liability,
but another person's asset.*
—Paul Krugman

OUT OF ALL THE ESSENTIAL BOOKKEEPING services business owners employ, long term liability is yet another one of the main concepts to review. Long term liabilities are a claim on the assets of a business and have a major impact on the financial health of an organization over time. This is especially true if the long-term liability for a company is poorly recorded and poorly managed. In small business accounting 101, we will show you how important these debts are for determining and preserving financial stability.

LONG TERM LIABILITY DEFINED

So what is a long term liability? Typically, long-term liability is considered to be any liability that is due in more than one year.

Companies often secure long-term loans in order to obtain important assets that will be used for an extended period of time.

Essential equipment, commercial facilities and company autos are all examples of long-term liability.

These are often recorded in the accounting records for the business as "bonds payable" or "long-term notes payable".

They require a transfer of assets by a specific date as due payment for a purchase or action that has already occurred.

LONG TERM LIABILITY MANAGING

While there are many topics that you will cover in Accounting 101, few are as valuable as accounting 101 long term liability and how to manage it properly.

This financial report gives businesses a comprehensive understanding of their overall financial well-being.

Adding the business owner's equity to the short and long-term liability for the business will reveal the company's total assets or net worth.

Using the chart of accounts to list long-term liability is a topic that is commonly explored in Accounting 101.

LONG TERM LIABILITY TYPES

There are long term liabilities and there are short term liabilities. All debts that are due and payable within the year are considered to be short-term liability or current liability.

Principal balances with a repayment period greater than 12 months are long-term liability. These two debts together represent the total liability for the business.

LONG TERM LIABILITY FUNCTION

Accounting 101 is so much more than learning to simply crunch numbers.

As a business owner you need to develop the ability to discern what these numbers mean for the future of your business and whether each debt or gain represents an opportunity for growth and increased financial health.

Short-term liability can be both positive and negative in that it can be representative of essential expenses for necessary portions of the operation or frivolous expenses that add no value the company.

When it comes to long-term liability, however, many of these debts are representative of items that perform positive functions for the business.

Not only might these items be critical for the maintenance of the operations overall, but these could contribute significantly to the growth and health of the business as shown on accounting 101 the income statement as well.

LONG TERM LIABILITY SUCCESS

Those who succeed in gaining a comprehensive understanding of long-term liability in Accounting 101 will ultimately have the ability to determine the long-term impacts of a major purchase.

This can be critical when creating detailed reports concerning spending and expected returns on the related investments.

Excessive long-term liability can cause a business to become overwhelmed.

Therefore an important learning aspect in understanding your company's finances is how to identify disproportionate borrowing and returns so that company leaders can be notified.

LONG TERM LIABILITY SUMMARY

Modest and well-managed borrowing for assets that produce substantial returns can result in increased financial health.

Moreover, low-interest rates and manageable payments can allow for the acquisition of larger buildings and more innovative forms of equipment that will lead to expansion, increased profits and an improved bottom line.

Recognizing that maintaining a balance between assets and overall liability is essential for establishing and maintaining financial stability.

SMALL BUSINESS ACCOUNTING 101 CONCLUSION

Now that you are over the initial hurdle and learning curve, keeping up with these accounting and bookkeeping basics will be easy!

> *If you enjoyed reading this book, I'd appreciate it if you would take a couple of minutes to post a short review at Amazon. Intelligent reviews help other customers make better buying choices. And because I read all my reviews personally, they will help me to write better books in the future. Thanks for your support!*

ADDITIONAL RESOURCES

www.Bookkeeping-Basics.net/accounting-definitions-glossary.html

www.Bookkeeping-Basics.net/accounting-definitions-wordsearch.html

www.Bookkeeping-Basics.net/accounting-definitions-ecourse.html

www.facebook.com/HorneFinancialServices

www.twitter.com/hornefncl

www.pinterest.com/hornefncl

NOTES

Copyright © 2018 by Stephanie Horne

All rights reserved. This book or any portion thereof may not be reproduced or used in any manner whatsoever without the express written permission of the publisher except for the use of brief quotations in a book review.

Printed in the United States of America

First Printing, 2018

ISBN 9781724084958

www.ingramcontent.com/pod-product-compliance
Lightning Source LLC
Chambersburg PA
CBHW030516220526
45464CB00006B/2823